BIGFOOT, UFO'S & The PARANORMAL

TRUE ENCOUNTERS
-Volume One -

PAUL G BUCKNER

Claremore, OK

ISBN- 978-1-7377772-1-2

DEDICATION

When in the courtroom, attorneys may call upon a witness to provide testimony. There are two kinds of witnesses - expert witnesses and factual witnesses. Both are important, but what is the difference? The answer is quite simple. An expert witness provides information concerning evidence provided in their field of study. They could be doctors, anthropologists, epidemiologists, and so forth.

An example could be a dentist called upon to provide expert testimony on the evidence presented concerning dental records. In comparison, a factual witness provides known facts. They saw things or knew things that others may not be privy to.

It is then up to the attorneys to comb through the testimony and find discrepancies. In other words, see the holes and exploit them to paint a complete picture and get to the truth. Both are extremely important. The possibilities are endless, and the truth is not always easy to find.

This series is dedicated to those that seek the truth.

CONTENTS

1

BIGFOOT TERRORIZES FARMER'S WIFE

My experiences began many years ago as a kid growing up in the country, running the fields and woods, exploring the creeks, lakes, and rivers.

It was 1979, and I had just turned eleven when I had my first encounter. I suppose I probably shouldn't say *my* encounter as it wasn't *my* encounter. Not exactly anyway. It was my aunt's, but it *was* my first experience. My *encounter* would happen years later.

I was born the middle child of three. My brother was three years older, and my sister was a few years younger. I didn't spend much time with either of them growing up. They had their friends, and I had mine. We grew up in the country on my granddad's original Cherokee allotment land in northeast Oklahoma. It was ten miles outside of town, but many neighbors were nearby, and most of them seemed to have kids. There was a whole pack of us wildlings that ran the woods, swam the creeks, and ripped up the dirt roads, terrorizing the local livestock with our summer excursions while enjoying every ounce of summer we could squeeze in before school started back up. One such popular venue, the Evansville Creek, lay to the north, less than a mile away from my house. Summers would find most neighborhood kids at a spot along the banks that we referred to as the Rock Hole. We called it that because of a massive gray rock that sat on the far side. You could often see the top of the enormous gray slab-rock as it ran along about ten feet parallel with the opposite bank. The only time the rock wasn't visible was when there had been a lot of rain. We would swim over to it, climb on top and jump off. A hole in the middle of it ran front to back under the surface, and we would dive under and swim through to the other side. It was a rite of passage, and it was more than a little scary in that murky creek water. It was our favorite place to be during the scorching hot days of summer, and we looked forward to it every year.

I hung out a lot with my cousin, who lived nearby. He was my age, and we spent most summers together when we were kids- up until his parents bought a farm and built a new house further away. We couldn't wait for school to be out for summer break because we had big plans to get together and camp out on the creek, fishing and swimming the entire time. It wasn't until we were out of school that we learned that our parents had other plans for us.

Our dads were brothers and came from a family of thirteen. Yup, eleven brothers and sisters, two girls and nine boys, and each had kids. All but one, anyway. To say that I had a large family is an understatement.

My dad was a master carpenter by trade, and most of my uncles worked in construction. One of my uncles was a heavy equipment operator and ran dozers and backhoes. He did the excavation work along with my cousin Steve. My dad and my uncles could build a house from the ground up, framing to roofing. They could do it all.

Times were different back then. In those days, men could do just about anything. They had to be self-sufficient. My dad could rebuild an engine, plant and harvest crops, raise livestock, train horses, and hunt and fish like Davy Crockett. They had to be able to do those things just to survive. He was the most competent man I've ever known. He was my hero. I can't ever remember a time that he ever missed a day of work. He was old school. No matter how he felt, he got up every day and went to work. He had no choice. There were times when I knew he didn't feel well or had suffered some kind of injury, but he still managed to drag himself to work every day. He didn't have healthcare other than the Indian hospital, and he hated to go. That meant time missed at work.

Summer arrived that year by entirely skipping spring. Or it sure seemed that way to us kids. One day it was sixty degrees, and the next, it was in the nineties. My big plan to spend as much time with my cousin as I could at the creek fell by the wayside the first morning of summer vacation.

Our small two-bedroom house was light green with a dark brown roof that faced east. When my dad started building it, I was only three or four years old, and we had just moved back from Kansas City. I still remember playing nearby while he worked on it. I was about five years old when we actually moved in,

I shared a bedroom with my brother back then. It was small but adequate for a couple of scrawny boys. A dresser with a mirror sat against a wall and a set of bunk beds opposite. My brother got the top bunk, of course. He was older, bigger, and just a bit ornerier than me. He got his way most of the time.

Our bedroom was pitch black on the morning dad woke us. He was never gentle about it. He just opened our door, flipped on the overhead light, and growled, "Get up!" So, we got up. We never lingered. We jumped up, got dressed, and received our marching orders for the day.

I suppose the thing that passed through my mind that morning was that he had a list of chores for us to do while he was at work. That was typical, so I wasn't too concerned about anything new. Clean our room, take care of the feeding and watering, then stay outside, oh, and don't wake mom who worked the night shift. Of course, it also went without saying, rule number one, don't get into trouble. Easy enough. Usually.

When I walked into the living room that morning, Dad was already heading out the door. I remember standing there just staring at him, wondering if I was expected to know what I was supposed to be doing at 6 a.m. It was all a bit confusing. Maybe he thought we still had school and was making sure we didn't miss the bus. I was surprised when he just said, "Let's go." I was even more surprised to see my brother getting on his bicycle and pedaling off down the dirt road. *Did I do something to get into trouble and couldn't remember? Am I being punished for it?* I was too scared to ask out loud. It wasn't that he was mean. He wasn't. He was just a no-nonsense type of person. Terse in his communication, but not mean, unless you did something wrong. Then, he became a bear, but that's another story.

When I got in the truck and watched my brother ride away, I got up enough courage to ask, "Where's Mike going?"

Dad said, "He has a job this summer working on the other side of the creek." I learned later that he was doing yard work and gardening for an elderly lady. "You're going with me to help at the job site."

Ah, man! I remember thinking. *This sucks.* I had big plans. I wanted to go to the creek, ride my bike, work on my fort down by the pond, hang out with my friends, anything but work with Dad. I did feel a little better about the trip when he told me my cousin would be there too.

Though not what I wanted to hear, it did make me feel a little better about the situation. I had often been to job sites during summers, but I never had to work. Not really. Cleaning up scraps was my regular job, and I always got to keep most of them. We used the scraps of wood to build our fort. It was a rickety, dangerous thing, but we didn't care. We were indestructible.

We arrived at the job site within a half hour. It was a typical house that my dad contracted with the Housing Authority of the Cherokee Nation to build. I saw my cousin was already there and dragging out equipment from the bed of my uncle's truck.

Dad told me to get out and give him a hand, then come inside because he had more things for me to do. I hopped out and pitched in. We had it unloaded in no time, and our dads began working on the house. Even though they asked us to do little things throughout the day, we got a lot of downtime for just hanging out and being kids. It was more fun than I thought it might be.

After lunch that day, a man who lived across the road from where our dads were working hurried over looking for my uncle. I remember the time because we had already eaten lunch and were working again.

"Where's your dads?" the guy asked. We could tell something was wrong from his worried expression and demeanor.

"They're inside," my cousin said, pointing toward the kitchen area of the new house. I think my dad was in the back running a saw.

We figured if they wanted us to know anything, they'd

come to tell us, so we continued playing. A few minutes later, I heard my dad say, "Get in the truck!"

We didn't hesitate. I remember the worried look on their faces, but I don't recall if my dad explained anything to me on the way. He did say that we had to get to their house right away because something happened to my aunt.

My aunt was a housewife and lived in a remote area about 20 miles outside of town called England Hollow. She was at home with my cousin's little sister, who was about eight years old. Something had happened, and she called the neighbor next door to the house our dads were working on to ask him to send my uncle home. This was the late '70s, so there were no cell phones. Everyone had landlines, most of which were party lines so, everyone knew everyone else's business in the county.

We hurried to the door when we got to their house, but my aunt had locked it. All the lights were off, and there was no sign of my aunt or my cousin. My uncle used his key to open the door, ran to the back bedroom, and found them hiding. They all came back in the living room, but my uncle now had two rifles in his hand. He handed one to my dad.

My aunt was crying, scared, and shaking. My cousin was hanging on to her mom and wouldn't let go. We all went to the living room to listen to her story.

"I was hanging out the laundry in the back yard when I saw it," my aunt said. "At first, I thought it might be a cow standing in the pasture, but as it got closer, I could tell that it was walking upright like a man. I thought it could be someone looking for their cows, so I kept hanging laundry."

I could see the fear still in her eyes as she spoke. She was visibly shaking. Anyone that knew my aunt knows that she didn't lie or make things up. She was a devout Christian lady and raised her kids not to lie. I believed her.

"I'd look up, and it would be a little closer like it was

watching me. That made me nervous, but I wasn't afraid. It was still quite a ways off, so I couldn't make out any features." She swallowed hard and gasped for air. Just listening to her made me a little scared because she kept looking out the windows like it might be lurking outside, whatever *it* was.

"I reached into the laundry basket, hung another shirt on the line, and noticed that it wasn't there anymore. I looked around the pasture and didn't see it anywhere. Then I heard this terrible racket coming from the barn. I've never heard anything like it before. I turned and looked, thinking someone was stealing a chicken or something. I still don't believe what I saw. It, the thing, was in the barnyard and had caught up one of the calves and slung it over its shoulder, stepped over the fence, and ran into the woods."

"Who was it? Did you get a good look at him?" my uncle asked.

"It wasn't a *him*. It was an *it*!" she exclaimed. "It was covered in black hair from head to toe, and it was huge. It was so big that it had to duck down through the barn door. It turned and looked right at me."

The barn door was seven feet tall. It was open so that the calves could go in and out of the little corral.

She almost passed out again just from telling the story. I remember the look of fear on her face, and she shook while telling us what happened. I didn't think she wasn't lying then, and I've never questioned her story since, especially after what we found at the barn later.

My uncle looked over at my dad.

"If it got one of my calves, we'd better go see if we can find it."

"Which way did it run off?" my dad asked.

"The same way it came, down the back pasture and into the woods. It carried that calf on its shoulders like it was a rag doll. Its face, oh my God, the eyes. It was terrible. I was scared stiff, scared out of my wits. As soon as I could, I ran inside and locked all the doors. It grunted at me a few more times before disappearing back the way it came. We hid in the bedroom until you got here. I didn't know if it was coming back."

We hurried to the barn, leaving my aunt in the house. When we got there, my uncle counted the calves, and sure enough, one was missing, but there was no damage to the fence. The gate was closed. We did, however, find big footprints. We hunted the rest of the day but never seen the creature or the calf again.

I don't remember much else about that day, and we never talked about it again, and eventually, it faded away and was all but forgotten.

That was my first experience, but it wouldn't be my last. I was fascinated.

2

PACIFIC NORTHWEST

Witness: *John R. McNary*
Interview Date: *August 12, 2020*
Location: Small Roadside Diner
      (*As told in his words, edited for clarity*)

"My name is John R. McNary. My friends call me Rake or John R. I'm a professional hunting and fishing guide by trade and freelance for several different outfitters throughout the year.

"I grew up in the woods where hunting and fishing were a way of life. I want to say that I hail from a particular town, but my parents were nomads, moving from town to town following work. I attended more schools than I care to remember.

"My dad worked in the logging industry, and my mother was an accountant. I, too, worked in logging for several years alongside my dad when I was younger, but I wouldn't say I liked it. I wouldn't say I liked anything to do with destroying the forests, to be honest. Don't get me wrong. I realize that a certain amount of management is necessary. Still, the rate at which we destroy our environment needs put in check, and more efforts put into the conservation and sustainable resources, in my opinion. I love the outdoors, and I make a living from it, but we should be respectful of our environment and make sure that we leave enough of it behind for future generations to enjoy. Sorry, that's my soapbox," Rake laughs.

Rake is a big guy standing at least six-foot-three, maybe four. He is built like a linebacker. I figured he could certainly take care of himself in the woods.

"Sarah and I live with our two dogs, a bloodhound named Rusty and a rottweiler. That's Big Jake. I have two step-daughters, Lisa and Kari. They're both married and raising their own families. Both of my folks passed away several years ago. We live in a small town where I work as a hunting guide on a local ranch. Our little place sits on the eastern edge of the Cherokee Nation Reservation in Oklahoma. It's a beautiful area surrounded by lakes and thousands of acres of hardwood forests." (*As I'm writing this, I've learned Rake has since moved to Texas and took a job with another outfitter.*)

I am familiar with the area and have traveled most of it myself, if not hunted or fished it as well. Rake asked a few questions, but I steered him back to avoid losing focus on his story.

"The only problem is, I spend so much time in the woods guiding for others that I rarely get to enjoy time at home. I go where the money is and that keeps me moving. I guess I caught some of that nomad from my folks. I keep telling myself that I'll slow down someday, but the truth is, we love traveling across the country and visiting new places, and meeting new people. It works for us. I work for a few different outfitters during the seasons, year-round, but we always find time for my passion, looking for Bigfoot. First, I firmly believe a Bigfoot-type creature lives in the woods and mountains of North America and is incredibly elusive and intelligent. It's not merely a belief, but I know for a fact that they exist. I had two encounters in different parts of the country, one in the pacific northwest when I was ten and another as an adult while on a camping trip with my wife in Arkansas. There, one of them got a little too close for comfort."

"Are you Cherokee?" I asked.

"Yes, on my mother's side. She grew up in Vian, Oklahoma," he said.

"Very cool. Was she traditional?"

"Not really," he answered. "But Mom went to school at Northeastern in Tahlequah, took a job in Kansas when she graduated, and that's when she met my dad. I guess they moved to the PNW soon after. I can't really remember that far back since we moved so much after I came along. We lived in Washington state around the time I was nine until about twelve or so.

"My dad was big into hunting and fishing, so I naturally gravitated to it. I was ten years old the year I got my first deer rifle, a Marlin 30/30. I couldn't wait to get in the woods and bag a deer with it. Now, I realize that a lot of folks would be thinking, 'You were only ten years old with a gun? On your own?' All I can say is, times were very different when I was growing up. I was raised around guns. Hunting and fishing were a way of life for us, and Dad taught me how to safely handle weapons very early - the greatest lesson of all - muzzle direction. Never aim at anything you don't want to kill. Period. Besides, I never hunted alone during those early years. My dad and I would always go out together. He'd find a good place for me to sit, usually near a game trail or watering hole. As I grew older, he taught me the art of still hunting, which directly contrasts with what the name implies."

Still hunting is about stealth, walking your prey's habitat with frequent stops for lengthy periods to scan and listen for the game. This method is effective in large tracts of land that may be unfamiliar or impractical to use a blind or tree-stand. It is necessary to become a skilled tracker and learn the habits of animals to stalk in all types of terrain such as woods, marshes, thick undergrowth, or overgrown fields using the wind to their advantage. There is an art to the method, but I will not divert as this isn't a How to Hunt tutorial.

I nod my understanding, and he continues.

"On this particular morning, we left the house an hour or so before dawn. Since we lived in a small place several miles from the nearest house, we had public hunting land all around us, hundreds of acres all to ourselves to hunt. It wasn't long before we got to the spot where I was to sit. We didn't have the fancy tree-climber deer stands like we have today. We found a good place to sit that would give us a good view all around. Usually, that consisted of a big tree for a backrest on a ridge or something along those lines. I settled in, and my dad said he would walk on down to a spot near the small creek branch a few hundred yards away. We hunted from sunup to sundown. The only time we came in during that time was if one of us bagged an elk or a deer. We didn't trophy hunt. We hunted to fill the freezer and feed the family.

"I settled in at the base of a big tree about halfway up the side of a small hill. My vantage point overlooked a convergence of a couple of game trails that wound around the bottom area, with trees scattered throughout. I had a hundred-and eighty-degree viewpoint with my back to the hillside, and I could see for a few hundred yards below me. Though there were lots of trees, there wasn't any undergrowth to speak of. I sat still as a statue, as well as a ten-year-old boy could, I guess," he laughed.

"I watched squirrels playing near me, and at one point, a coyote walked across the bottom. It never saw me. A few does played near me, but I only had a tag for a buck, so I left them alone. They soon left, and I was in for the long haul now, just waiting patiently. Though I was vigilant, I'm sure I daydreamed and tried to occupy my time with thoughts of who knows what. I had blended into the forest and was still and quiet. The animals had no clue; to them, I was just another bush or tree.

"It must have been getting close to noon when I got a weird feeling. I didn't know what it was at first, but it felt like someone was watching me. I thought it might be my dad coming to find me, but I ruled that out because I knew he would have already made his presence known. He wouldn't sneak up on me, or anyone with a gun for that matter. I noticed the woods had gone quiet. I didn't see any more animals around, no deer, coyotes, wolves, nothing at all. I never moved. I was still as a statue the whole time. Getting quite stiff and achy, but I never moved, not my body anyway. I may have been a little scared; I don't know. Using nothing but my eyes, I scanned all-around below, slowly, back and forth, picking out every little thing looking for the one thing that didn't belong. A small sapling that I noticed earlier with only a few leaves that dangled from its branches too stubborn to fall, a clump of small evergreens, an old laydown where a dead tree finally gave way to gravity, but nothing out of the ordinary. But then, I saw something different - a slight movement.

"At first, I just thought it was nothing more than the wind blowing a leaf or twig. It wasn't until I steadied my gaze on the area that the complete picture started coming into view. I focused on a large tree that I had looked at several times that morning. There appeared to be long, stringy moss growing on one side. It fluttered in the breeze that swirled in that bottom. I relaxed a moment and breathed a sigh of relief. I was scaring myself. I must've blown out a breath or made some sound because the moss I was watching suddenly disappeared. I couldn't believe my eyes. *Had the wind shifted directions,* I asked myself. The moss just moved behind the tree. Then I heard it. It was a deep, guttural grunt followed by a weird, nasally whistle. I remember snapping my head around slightly to see around another tree that was blocking my sight path. Suddenly the earth shook. This huge- *monster* leaped out of that tree and hit the ground so hard that I felt the impact. The ground shook, and I heard the heavy thud. The thing took off and ran with incredible speed and agility, crossed the forest floor in seconds, and was gone.

"I was in shock. I couldn't believe what I just saw. Not only was I in shock and disbelief, but I was also scared out of my mind. This thing was huge, covered in hair from head to toe, a monster bigger than anything I could ever have imagined. How long had it been there, watching me?

"I'll tell you now. I was one scared kid. It never occurred to me to aim my rifle at it. The only thing going through my mind, I guess, was fear. I'm not sure how much time passed before my dad found me.

"When he got to me, I was trembling, still shaking. He asked me if I got too cold, but I told him no and explained what I saw. I had never been so glad to see him.

He didn't call me out for making up a story or anything. He asked me to tell him exactly what I saw. Then he insisted that we go down to the bottom and look around. I refused, so he told me to stay right there.

After maybe twenty minutes, Dad came back up and said he didn't see anything. No tracks or indications of anything that could have been there. He made me promise never to speak of it to anyone and, most especially, to my mom.

"That was my first experience with Sasquatch, and it wouldn't be my last. In the years that followed, I became more and more interested in cryptozoology and have made it an extensive hobby."

"Wow," I said. "I'm sure that was a terrifying experience, especially for a ten-year-old boy. I'm not sure what I would have done in your situation. So, the thought never occurred to you to shoot it?"

"No, it never even crossed my mind. It happened too fast."

"Did you hunt there the next day or anytime afterward?" I studied Rake's face for any emotion.

"Yeah, but I can't remember if we went back out the next day or not. I know we hunted the rest of that season, but Dad stayed close. We never mentioned it to my mom."

"I was going to ask you about that," I said.

"Yeah, Dad thought it best not to worry her, I suppose. She probably had enough to worry about with her kid carrying a gun. I was a hellion, to be honest. I think I was in trouble most of my childhood." He laughed at that.

I never got the impression that he was lying or making any part of it up. Why would he?

"So, tell me about the time something harassed you when you and your wife were camping," I said.

"That was a hell of a trip," Rake started. "It was only a few years ago, too, 2016. It was just a camping trip near a place called Devil's Den in Arkansas. Early fall. We camped in the primitive area but a little more back in there."

"We?" I asked.

"Yeah, sorry. My wife was with me. No hunting, just camping and a little fishing. Anyway, it was getting late in the day, and it got dark pretty early in the fall. I had caught a few brownies and had them on a stringer in the edge of the water. I tied it off on a tree limb that hung out over the water. I had walked off down the creek still fishing when I thought I heard something. Some rocks shuffling or something, but I didn't see anything so, I really didn't pay attention to it, to be honest. I figured it would get too dark on me a few minutes later, and I still had a pretty good hike back to camp. I fished a little while longer before I called it. When I went to get my fish, they were gone, stringer and all."

"Obvious question. Was it tied good, or did you have it looped over something?" I asked.

"No, I had it tied good to that tree limb. There's no way that it could have just come loose. Impossible. Not without opposable thumbs," Rake laughed.

"Do you think it could have been someone messing with you? Maybe someone that was camped near you or something? I know that area well, have ridden both horses and four-wheelers all over. There are lots of people there year-round," I said.

Rake shook his head, "No. At first, I thought that might be the case, but I looked everywhere and didn't see anyone around. I scouted down the creek trail, but nothing. That spot was pretty secluded. That's why I hiked there. It wasn't the usual place that someone would go, but I also understand that if *I'm* there, anyone else could have been too. But, as I said, I searched the area good. They would have to have been watching me to know that the fish were there, and if it were a person, then it becomes a question of why? Why would they steal my fish? Not to mention that I wasn't more than fifty feet away. I think I would have seen them at some point. Anyway, I was pissed. I was looking forward to some fish for supper, and I had just enough. I think I yelled a few profanities out there," he laughed. "I'm sure the trees cared."

"Did you get any response?" I asked with a chuckle.

"No. Not that I recall. I wasn't thinking Bigfoot at the time. I was thinking it was probably some sneaky jerk messing with me. I thought possibly a raccoon, but still, I think I would have seen it."

"Yeah, I get you. I may have thought the same thing," I said. "So, what did you do then?"

"It was late in the evening and would be getting dark soon, so I had no choice but to go back empty-handed. When I told my wife what happened, she gave me a puzzled look. Then she told me that while I was gone, she heard some strange noises nearby. It came from further out in the woods. She felt it might have been other campers out for a walk but assumed they were too far away to make out what they were saying.

"So, that evening, we grilled a couple of pork steaks and kicked back by the fire, just relaxed, you know? Didn't think any more about it. Not sure what time it was when we turned in, but it was pretty late, after midnight anyway.

My wife is a heavy sleeper, but I wake up at the slightest noise. Something woke me around 2:30 a.m. I remember because I looked at my watch when I heard it. It was a scratching sound, like if you ran your fingers down the side of a nylon tent. Something was out there.

"I sleep with my .45 within reach, always have, always will, just a habit. I sat up slowly and grabbed it in case an animal was out there. Not a lot of bears in the area, but there have been some over the years. Just can't be too careful. I slowly unzipped the tent flap, just kind of eased it open enough to see out. There wasn't much light from the stars but enough to make out something moving near the fire. Of course, there wasn't a fire any longer, just ashes with some hot coals underneath.

"I had a flashlight with me when I went to bed, so I felt around for it. I certainly wasn't about to shoot at somebody in the dark. That's just all kinds of stupid. But I was ready to protect us if it came to that. Why would anybody in their right mind want to try to rob someone's camp? It's not like we had anything of great value laying around, just a couple of fishing poles, a couple of coolers, you know, camp stuff. Anyway, I started groping around looking for that flashlight when I guess I must've made too much noise. When my hand finally wrapped around it and I turned to unzip the tent all the way, I heard this heavy grunt. It's hard to describe, but it was like a heavyweight fighter getting punched in the gut when he's not ready, loses all his wind. I shined my light outside and jumped through the tent opening at the same time. I was a split-second too late. Whoever was out there was gone in a flash. I shined my light all around but didn't see anything.

"My wife heard the commotion by then, and she poked her head out and asked me what was going on. I told her that I scared an animal away that had been poking around the camp looking for food. I didn't want her worrying about anything, but I'll tell you this - there were at least twenty feet from that fire to the edge of the woods. Whoever or whatever was out there was an Olympic sprinter to cover that distance in only the two or three seconds it took me to step out and shine my light."

I asked, "Did you hear any more sounds? Like running in the woods, footsteps, that sort of thing?"

"No, nothing. I thought that whoever it was had ducked behind a bush and stopped or was gone for good. I sat up a bit longer to keep watch, but I dozed off. I slept for half an hour or so. When I woke, I stood, stretched, and was ready to head back into the tent when I saw this weird light in the woods."

"Weird light?" I asked.

"Yeah. It was a dull white light out in the middle of the

woods. My first thought was, *there you are. I found you now, buddy.* I thought it was someone's flashlight, and there was a good chance it was the person that had been in our camp snooping around. But, as I watched it, it didn't act like a person holding a flashlight. It was stationary for a few seconds, and then it slowly lifted straight up like it was climbing a tree or something. I knew it wasn't a flashlight when it started moving because it should have been going in and out, aiming in different directions, kind of herky-jerky in a person's hand. This was just a steady glow broken up only by the limbs that must've been between it and me. It floated up, then over, then up, down, just a slow-moving, almost bouncing-like action. Then another one appeared beside it. I must've watched that action for several minutes before it floated up and finally disappeared. It was the creepiest thing I've ever seen. I couldn't tell how big the light was or how far away it was. It could've been the size of a basketball or ping-pong ball fifty-feet away or five-hundred. In the dark, you have no reference point for size or distance.

"I went back to bed after that. I didn't see or hear anything else the rest of the night, but I slept in a little later than I had intended. I wanted to start fishing again early and be back before my wife got up and started fixing breakfast. She was already up when I finally rolled out. I smelled coffee. When I got dressed and put my boots on, she handed me a cup and asked me about last night's commotion. As I said, though, I didn't want her to be scared or worry, so I didn't tell her about everything. Not at that time anyway.

"We stayed a couple of days longer, but nothing else happened after that night. I never saw a sign that anyone had been around anymore until we were packed and ready to go. I did a last-minute check to ensure we had everything loaded and hadn't left any trash behind or forgotten anything. That's when I saw it. A rock cairn, stacked from big to small, about seven rocks high, no more than twenty feet from the camp. It could have been there for days, I suppose, but I don't think so. I believe it was built the night that everything happened, and we just never noticed it before. No idea why or what it meant, but very peculiar."

"What're your thoughts or best guess as to what it meant?" I asked.

"No idea. Maybe whoever stole my fish left it as an apology for stealing them, or maybe it was a sign left for others to stay away. No idea."

Rake's encounter was not unlike the hundreds of other stories told by witnesses around the country. The central theme seems to be more curiosity by these creatures than anything else. I have yet to encounter anyone injured as a direct result of an attack. Many have reported indirect injuries, such as trips and falls trying to run away after being scared. However, there have been many people that have gone missing without a trace in the forests. Is there a connection between these missing persons and Sasquatch? It's possible, but I believe it's unlikely with so many more encounter stories that involved no physical attack whatsoever.

3

NATIVE AMERICAN LORE

In the old days, animals could speak and were held in the same regard as man, living and working alongside one another in harmony. At the beginning of time, the creator told all animals and people to stay awake and fast for seven days and seven nights. Though all tried diligently, some fell asleep on the first night while others held out longer. By the seventh night, only the owl and panther remained awake. They were gifted with the power to see in the dark and prey upon others who slept at night. The cedar, spruce, and pine were also still awake and were gifted with never needing to sleep; they would forever be green and awake. They had strong medicine. The creator punished the other trees for their lack of endurance and said they must go back to sleep each winter and lose their beautiful leaves.

Every story changes over time and takes on new shapes and meanings. It evolves from one teller to the next. For instance, if ten people listen to a storyteller and then go out and re-tell that same story, each one will tell it differently. Though the basis of the story may remain intact, which is critical to the lesson, the nuances are bound to fluctuate.

Our culture is shaped through the telling of our stories. Values, morals, and character are embedded within them, but keep in mind that not every story is based on a truth or told as a parable, folklore, or legend. As with any culture, some stories are nothing more than that, a story, and are often created to be entertaining or told to scare children into behaving.

One of my favorite stories, when I was a young boy, was the Cherokee story of how Opossum lost the hair on his tail.

In the beginning, Opossum had a beautiful long and bushy tail and was very proud of it. He sang many songs about it. Rabbit didn't have a tail and was very jealous. Being a trickster by nature, Rabbit played a dirty trick on Opossum. Rabbit planned a big party during the council and invited all the other animals. When Rabbit asked Opossum to come, Opossum said he would only attend if he could have a special seat where all the others could see him and his beautiful tail. He was always bragging about his tail and took every opportunity to show it off.

Rabbit knew he would say this and planned accordingly. Rabbit told Opossum that he would send Cricket to take special care of his tail to prepare for the party.

Cricket was a good friend to Rabbit and was also known as an excellent barber. When he arrived at Opossum's the following day, he said, "I'm here to prepare your glorious tail for the party."

Opossum was pleased to hear this and invited Cricket in, stretched himself out, and closed his eyes to allow Cricket to work. Cricket worked feverishly, getting Opossum's tail ready. He first combed it out and then began to clip it and shape it, but he quietly cut it all the way down to the skin. As Cricket finished, he carefully wrapped a ribbon around the tail to hold the loose hair in place. Opossum didn't know what the cricket was secretly doing. Through his pride and vanity, Opossum just knew that all the other animals would love the opportunity to see and appreciate his beautiful tail. He expected nothing less.

When the party began, Opossum arrived and found the seat promised him to display his beautiful tail for all to see. Soon, it was Opossum's turn to dance. He stood, stepped into the circle with a huge grin, and began to sing, "Look upon my beautiful tail," and he danced, swishing his tail wrapped in a shiny red ribbon back and forth. All the other animals shouted, and this pleased Opossum. His grin got even bigger, and he sang louder, "Look at my beautiful tail. Come and see the wonderful color of my tail. See how magnificent it is," he said, dancing gleefully.

The animals' shouts became louder, and finally, Opossum pulled the ribbon free and danced and sang louder. "Gaze upon the beauty of my tail, see how big and full it is and how the wind sweeps through it."

All the others suddenly began laughing. They laughed so hard that Opossum was confused. When he looked at their faces, he saw they were pointing at him, at his tail. When he turned to see, a look of horror spread over his face. Not a single hair remained on his once beautiful tail. It was as bare as that of Lizard. In his embarrassment, he rolled over and flung himself to the ground and played dead.

Now, even to this day, Opossum has a hairless tail and will roll over and play dead when he is caught by surprise.

This story is both entertaining and educational for native youth, a story of pride and consequences.

Often, stories fall victim to the shades of translation. In oral traditions, stories are passed down through generations. Even though the Cherokee had a written language for many years, these stories may not have been written down or are somewhat corrupted due to translation errors. New stories emerge.

There are many words in Cherokee that do not have a concise meaning in English. In many instances, there isn't one at all. An example, the English phrase *goodbye*, does not have an equivalent in Cherokee. Instead, we say Donadagohvi (Doh nah dah go huh ee), which means, "Until we meet again."

It is fascinating how closely some Native American legends compare with some of today's eyewitness accounts of Bigfoot. Many tribes have different names for the same creature. The Modoc call it Matah Kagmi or Yah'yahaas. The Choctaw has a few references, such as Champe, a giant or big hairy man-eater that smells overpowering. This could be a spirit but is often attributed to Bigfoot today. They also have a word, Hattak Lusa Chito, which means a large dark man. A witch reportedly brought this creature to Oklahoma from Mississippi, sending it to harass people he didn't like. The monster, or Bigfoot, was eventually freed after his master was murdered.

The Cherokees have a word that seems to come from a questionable source. The oldest written account of Tsul 'Kalu comes from a story by James Mooney in 1888-1897. The Cherokee Nation speakers I have talked to say the word has no meaning in this form. It seems to be missing letters, or Mooney got it wrong. There have been many variations found on the internet that attempt to spell out the pronunciation. The most prominent one seen is "sool-kuhlu," but this would be incorrect regardless of the missing letters. The "Ts" has a "J" sound, and the "U" is in the long-form. The word, Tsu, is pronounced with a soft "th" on the end of it. Thus, one would pronounce it, Joo(th)–Kaw–Lu, phonetically.

What is interesting about the word is that there is an area located in Jackson County, North Carolina, where a large boulder rests. The stone is inscribed with ancient drawings and is known as Judaculla Rock, a bastardization of the language? But, when said aloud, Judaculla or Tsul 'Kalu might sound similar. Archeologists that have studied the stone petroglyphs maintain they date back almost 3,000 years and have never been deciphered.

The legend of Tsul 'Kalu, as recounted by Mooney in his book, *History, Myths, and Sacred Formulas of the Cherokees,* is a story that warrants a closer examination. When the story is compared to eyewitness accounts of Bigfoot today, the parallels are remarkable. I have heard this story told only a few times, and it's different with each telling and each storyteller. I suspect it is because of the length and the many details.

As the story goes, a young woman of age to marry lived alone with her widowed mother. Her mother counseled her to be patient in settling for a husband. There was no need to rush. She should find a good hunter and provider to ensure that she and her daughter would be well cared for as times could be challenging, especially in the harsh winters of the Smokey Mountains.

The young woman slept alone in the asi outside the main home at night. An asi is the smaller, round, dome-shaped winter home used by the Cherokees. It was usually sank into the earth to help keep the warmth trapped inside.

One night, a stranger called on the young woman in

hopes of courting the girl. He was called Tsul 'Kalu. She made it clear to the caller that her mother would only allow her to keep the company of a great hunter. Declaring himself to be a great hunter, the girl let him inside, where he stayed the night. The great hunter left just before daybreak. When the morning came, the girl and her mother discovered a freshly killed deer waiting for them. This proved his claim of being a skilled hunter and his ability to provide for them.

He returned the following night and stayed with the girl but once again left just before daybreak. This time, two deer waited for them. The mother was delighted with her daughter's new husband but said she wished he would bring them some wood as winter was on them, and it was challenging to keep up with the need.

The following day, the woman discovered several large trees in front of the home, entire trees, including the roots. This angered the mother as this was of no use to them. She told her daughter that she wanted smaller wood that they could burn for cooking and heating. The following day, however, nothing waited for the pair. Instead, someone had cleared the land of the trees.

The girl said nothing of this to Tsul 'Kalu. Every night he stayed with her, but every morning he left before daybreak. The one constant was there was always a game animal waiting for the mother and her daughter. He was indeed a great hunter, but over time the girl's mother became frustrated. She desperately wanted to meet her new son-in-law. She had never met him or even seen him. The girl told her husband of this, but he did not want her mother to see him. She began to cry, and finally, he relented. However, he warned the girl that her mother must not say anything about his appearance.

When morning came, the girl brought her mother to the asi where her new husband lay. The mother peered in and saw a giant with long, slanting eyes and a sloping forehead. Covered in long hair from head to toe, Tsul 'Kalu was so large that he barely fit in the small asi. The mother fled and cried out, "Usga' se ti' yu," which means frightful.

The forest giant was enraged, and he left, vowing never to let the mother see him again. He returned to his homeland high in the mountains. After some time had passed, Tsul 'Kalu missed his bride greatly and returned to get her and bring her back to his home.

The girl had a brother who lived in another village. When he learned that she had a husband, he wanted to see her and meet his new brother-in-law. But, he was too late. They were gone. His mother explained what had happened. Feeling pity for his lonely mother, he went to find his sister in hopes of bringing her home. It was a long, arduous journey up the mountain, but it was easy to track his sister because Tsul 'Kalu was a giant and left enormous footprints on the ground. On the mountainside, there was a cave where he saw his sister and others dancing, but it was too steep for him to reach. He called out for his sister, and when she heard him, she recognized his voice and came down and met him. They visited for a long time that day, but he soon left as she would not invite her brother inside to meet her husband. He came back several times, and each time went away without ever having met him.

A few years later, the girl came home for a visit. Tsul 'Kalu was hunting nearby but said she and her husband would be leaving in the morning. If they wanted to see him before they left, come out early in the morning. If she and Tsul 'Kalu left before they got there, the great hunter would leave the meat for them. Morning came, but the giant and his bride were gone before they awoke. As promised, freshly killed deer were hanging. There was enough meat to feed the entire village. When the town learned this, they wanted to see the great Master of Game, Tsul 'Kalu.

Tsul 'Kalu, in a booming, unseen voice from the forest, spoke to his brother-in-law and told him that no one could see him until they were dressed in new clothes. He then instructed the people to meet in the communal house and fast for seven days. At the end of seven days, he would provide new clothes for everyone and allow everyone to see him. But, Tsul 'Kalu gave them a strict warning, no one was to leave the townhouse during the time of fasting or raise the war cry when he appeared.

The people gathered in the communal house and fasted for an entire week, but someone disobeyed the giant's orders. One among them - from another village - snuck out each night to get something to eat. On the seventh day, a thundering sound drew nearer. It was the sound of giant boulders crashing down the mountain. When the disobedient man heard this, he fled in fear and sounded the war cry. As soon as he did this, the sound disappeared. Tsul 'Kalu did not show up to reveal himself to the people.

The giant's brother-in-law returned to the mountain and asked why he did not come with the new clothes.

"I came with them, but you did not obey my word. You broke the fast and raised the war cry," Tsul 'Kalu answered,

The brother-in-law explained that it was a person from another village that had disobeyed. He pleaded with Tsul 'Kalu to reconsider, but the great hunter was not swayed.

"Now," Tsul 'Kalu said, "you can never see me."

It is easy to see the striking similarities of ancient Native American lore and the many encounters of Bigfoot today. Eyewitness accounts profess that Bigfoot is a large, bipedal creature covered in long hair standing anywhere from six to nine feet tall and weighing upwards of 600lbs. Often, Bigfoot is described as having a sloped or cone-shaped head. Many encounters have spoken of witnessing the creature kill fully-grown deer or other animals by simply breaking its neck with ease.

Many legends and myths are rooted in 'a' truth and embellished upon from teller to teller. Could this Cherokee story be about Bigfoot or Sasquatch kidnapping a beautiful maiden from a nearby village and taking her away into the mountains? Or is the story just that, a story?

In some instances, as with this story, I suspect that the person that recounted the tale to Mooney may have been humoring him, simply pulling his leg. No one knows for sure.

The description of slanted eyes and forehead to the enormous height and immense size of the beast and giant footprints all match descriptions of first-hand accounts given by thousands of people across the country of Bigfoot. There must be some accounting for the striking similarities. Is Sasquatch real or a spirit being?

4

KIAMICHI MOUNTAIN BIGFOOT

Witness: *Sam M.*
Interview Date: *January 22, 2019*
Location: *Honobia Creek*

I came across many interesting people in my travels and while researching. One such character was an elderly gentleman that lived in the Kiamichi Mountains of southern Oklahoma. His name was Sam.

Sam was a full-blood Cherokee born and raised in Oklahoma. His family was originally from a small community just outside of Sallisaw called Nicut. Sam taught me how to pronounce his Cherokee name and the meaning behind it. Though I wrote it down many years ago, I'm not sure if I have the spelling correct, and I do not possess the font type to spell it out in its original form. The meaning was relatively simple and, as he pointed out, not very interesting. When he was a young boy, he was thrown from a horse and suffered a leg injury. Though it was temporary, he walked with a slight limp for most of that summer. Sam fashioned a cane out of a small limb to use while he recovered. His grandmother called him what roughly translates to, *'Walks with a Stick.'*

In his later years, as when I knew him, he used a cane most of the time to get around. He said the injury never bothered him growing up, and he could still run just as fast as any of the other boys, but the limp became more pronounced when he was much older.

Sam was in his mid-seventies, but I would not have guessed him older than fifty to fifty-five at most. His mind was as sharp as a tack, and the sparkle in his eyes when he smiled gave not a hint of being any older. He had few wrinkles and was as strong as any man I ever knew. His hands were big and calloused from years of hard work but now crimped from arthritis. It wasn't until I had known him a while and shared stories with him that I learned his actual age. He credited his youthful appearance to living a simple life. He went to water every day, regardless of the weather. He was grateful for everything the creator had given him.

Sam married when he was a young man, and together, they raised two boys. I never had the pleasure of meeting his family, though I felt like I knew them just from Sam's stories he shared with me. His wife had passed on, and his sons had both married and moved away. Though they often visited when they were younger, those visits had decreased through the years, and I think it weighed on Sam's heart. He was lonely.

I loved hearing Sam's stories. He had some of the best, and I could sit and listen to him talk all night long. His smooth baritone voice never cracked, and his rhythm and cadence were perfect.

We always began by building a small fire in the back yard

to enjoy the evening air when I visited. Sometimes he would break out in song. It would be in his first language, so he would tell me a little about it when he finished and explain that he was praising the creator for something.

Sam was a fascinating gentleman. A proud Cherokee who lived primarily traditional. I say mostly because, even though he was a full-blood, a first language speaker, lived a simple life, and practiced the old ways, he still embraced the modern world. He enjoyed watching TV, and he loved ice cream. He kept his freezer full of it.

As we visited in his kitchen late one evening, he turned, grabbed my hand, and stared into my eyes without saying a word for the longest time. It seemed like he was looking inside me, into my very soul. Perhaps it was to see if he could trust me with his story. He had never done this before. Finally, he turned and walked outside and motioned for me to follow. He asked me to gather some wood and build a fire. He sat down, propped his hand-carved cane down on his chair, and waited patiently.

When the fire was blazing, he asked me to sit across from him. He said, "I have a story to share with you."

I could tell whatever he wanted to share with me was something of considerable weight, just the way he was acting. He wasn't his usual light-hearted self. He was more earnest and thoughtful. What he told me was one of the most exciting stories I had ever heard.

"This is a true story that happened many years ago," Sam said, slowly drawing his words out.

I sat down across from him with great anticipation. He took his time. I remember thinking at the time that he was overly dramatic to add excitement to what he was about to say. He was, after all, a storyteller and a damn good one.

Sam began to speak as the fire crackled, sending tiny red sparks into the pitch-black evening sky.

"My brothers and I used to hunt together when we were kids," he sighed heavily before continuing. "But that was a long time ago. When I was a young man having just returned home from the Army, I lived here with my mother and two brothers. They've all passed on now, but I remember it like it was only yesterday." He paused in reflection.

His story always stood out to me because, as fantastic as it seems, I never got the inclination that he was telling me anything other than the exact truth as he remembered it. It wasn't a story that elders told to keep kids in line. These events happened to my friend.

I sunk back in the fold-out lawn chair and got comfortable. Sam would tell his story at his pace, and I did not interrupt him.

"This was back in the '60s, you know," Sam began. "We didn't talk about the war when I got home. We never did. It was just something that happened. We did our part, and that was it.

Sam paused. He was remembering. I couldn't imagine the horrors that he must've seen in the Viet Nam. I could tell he struggled with it and what he had to do there, but he was also a proud veteran of serving his country. He told me his father served before him, and both of his brothers did as well, though one never made it home, and the other moved to California when he returned. They didn't hear from him much; he didn't keep in touch and passed years earlier.

Sam stood and picked up a small stick to poke at the fire. His shoulders sank, and he stooped a little more as he returned to his chair and slowly lowered himself down again. I noticed the wind had died down to a mere breeze, and the smoke from the fire drifted lazily into the night. The crackle of the burning wood was the only sound other than the elder's ragged breathing.

"When fall came, I was in the woods hunting. Everyday.

Just me and my bow. I made my bows out of bois d'arc. Made my own arrows too. Those were mostly hickory. I still do," Sam said, lifting his hands to look at them. "As much as I can anyway."

Sam held a great sense of pride in his bow-making. He'd shown me a few of his bows over the years and told me how he made them several times.

"I'd be up a few hours before the sun and fix a pot of coffee before heading out into the woods. I'd hunt all day. Sometimes I'd camp down by the river or one of the creeks and stay out for a few days at a time. I wasn't ever worried about the weather. I knew how to build a shelter and make a fire. I'm an Indian, you know," he said, laughing. Sam had a great sense of humor.

I was captivated by his stories. This one was no exception. I knew this was something he didn't tell many people, if any at all, just from the way he began. But I wanted him to get to the good stuff quickly though I held my tongue out of respect for my friend. He waited a moment to let his energy come back, and with a deep breath, he began again.

"That day, I hadn't planned on being gone very long. But like I said, sometimes I'd just stay in the woods. My mother must've heard me rustling around in the kitchen. She got up and cooked me some breakfast. She was a hard worker. Life wasn't handed to her on a silver plate," Sam said, shaking his head. "No, sir. She was the strongest woman I ever knew. She didn't talk much, but when she did, you listened, and we learned to do what she told us the first time," he said, chuckling. "I think she knew that I was not well yet. From the war, I mean. But she didn't know how to help me. I didn't know how, to be honest. But she could tell I was a different person then."

Off in the night, I heard a coyote howl followed by several yips. It was joined by several others a moment later. They were on the hunt. Sam cocked his head to listen. When they grew silent, he continued his story.

"After I ate breakfast, I gathered my things and told her that I might be out a few days. I didn't know. She just told me to be careful. That was it. I left. No one ever worried about me."

Sam shifted in his chair and reached out to warm his hands by the fire. I'm sure the warmth was soothing.

"I walked down the trail toward the river. It was cold that morning, but not much snow. Not yet, anyway. It was still dark when I left, but I had what we called a wheat lamp. It was a light with a strap that you adjusted to fit your head, and it ran off a battery you carried around your waist. It lasted a long time, and it kept your hands free to carry stuff; coon hunters used them. When I got to the river, I found my old johnboat, threw my stuff in, and shoved off. I had a place down the river a few miles that I liked to hike to. It was just easier traveling by boat instead of climbing up and down those ridges. There's some rough country in there." He gestured to the woods.

Sam stood and moved closer to the fire. He did this ever so often though he never moved fast. He seemed restless.

"The sun came up, but it was just gray skies. I could see the bank on each side of the creek. There were ducks on the water that flew off when they saw me. I saw other signs that the woods were waking up. Squirrels, hawks – you know, normal stuff. I saw a couple of small deer drinking and grazing near the water's edge at one point, but I was looking for a good buck. And to be honest, I wasn't ready to end my hunt before it even started," Sam laughed.

"It wasn't long before I pulled over to the other side and dragged my boat out onto the bank. The ground was frozen and covered in a thin layer of snow and ice. I fell a couple of times, but I was young then and bounced right back up. I slung my duffle on my back and started hiking. My place was way back where I used to camp with my brothers. I wanted to go there before I started hunting and set up camp. It was a few miles away, but the trails were good." He turned and looked into the darkness. "That's when I first noticed the change in the weather."

Sam paused long enough to stand and move closer to the fire. I took the opportunity to grab a couple more sticks and throw them on. Several embers scattered into the wind, dancing on the breeze along with a lot of smoke from the greenwood. Sam did a little dance and broke into one of his songs. It didn't last long, and he didn't explain. I didn't ask. If he wanted me to know, he would have told me. Finally, he turned back and continued.

"The further in I got," he began, "the darker it seemed to get. I guess I hadn't noticed earlier because when you're walking around in the woods, even in daylight, there are places where it's too dark to see. But this was different. The air was heavier, colder. Then it began snowing. I had my bow in my hand in case I saw a deer, and I walked softly. I was pretty stealthy in my youth. I'm a Cherokee warrior," Sam said, laughing. His smile stretched across his face. "I could sneak my way through the middle of a buffalo herd."

I laughed along at his joke, but I knew he meant it.

"The threat of snow didn't bother me – wasn't worried at all. I think I was grateful for it. Where I had been, I never saw snow. The beauty that the great creator gives us comes in all forms. I did hurry along, though, so that I could get to where I wanted to camp and get a lean-to built. It had been a few years since I had been in those woods, but I remembered my way and found the spot. A small creek ran nearby and fed the river with runoff from the mountain. There was an oxbow there. I found a nice clump of trees and dropped my duffle.

"I set about cutting some limbs and building a lean-to next to it. I had a small tarp and some rope with me. I didn't have a pup tent, but I wished I did. I remember thinking that would have been easier. Anyway, I got my shelter built and grabbed plenty of dead wood for a fire later. The snow wasn't heavy at that point - just specks of white floating down and settling on the ground. I was getting restless and decided it was time to do some hunting.

"I grabbed my bow and wandered down to the creek and followed it upstream. I found the ridge where my brothers and I would play and climbed up to the top. From there, you could see for miles. There was a little clearing below, and where I knew, there used to be a small pond. Animals would sometimes drink there while they grazed in that field. So, I sneaked down the hillside sticking to the tree line. I made it down to it, then found a nice little spot hidden away where I couldn't be seen and waited. I must've just daydreamed the afternoon away because I didn't remember seeing anything. Not that first day anyway.

"I made my way back to my camp as it was getting dark and set about building a fire. That took the longest. I was cold, and building a fire with frozen fingers was challenging but not a problem. Did I tell you I'm an Indian?"

He laughed - a big drawn-out laugh from deep down. His eyes gleamed in the firelight as the flames licked at the night sky. It was good to hear him laughing.

"After I got a fire going, I sat in the lean-to and just, I dunno, prayed a lot. Us vets back then didn't have any help when we came home. A lot of my friends turned to a bottle to cope with the war. I turned to the woods. That was my place of healing. Where I felt comfortable, I guess. Safe maybe. I had to find more wood to keep the fire going all night, but that gave me something to do and stay busy. I finally laid down and slept. I had weird dreams. Usually, they were about the war, but not on that night. I can't recall exactly what they were, but I remember they weren't of ordinary things - more like visions."

Sam sighed heavily and took a deep breath.

"The next morning, I woke up cold. My fire burned down to coals, so I got that going again, dug through my mess kit, and made some coffee. Then I grabbed my bow and quiver, climbed over the ridge again, and headed for that clearing. Just as I got there, I saw two nice bucks step out into the open. I drew my bow and let an arrow fly before they saw me. They weren't more than forty feet away, and I shot the closest one. It ran only a few yards away, and the other one took off back into the woods. I drew my knife and gutted my deer, threw it over my shoulders, and started making my way back to camp. And that's when I saw it for the first time."

Sam locked eyes with me again. I could see he was dead serious when he spoke those following words.

"Not more than twenty feet away on the trail that I had just come down stood a giant of a monster." Sam stood and held his arms near the fire.

"It had long, coarse reddish-black hair from head to toe, reminding me of a sheepdog. It towered over me. Had to be at least eight, maybe nine feet tall," he said, reaching above his head to indicate how big it was. "It stared straight at me. Its eyes were sunken and dark under a heavy brow, black and piercing but red all around, bloodshot. Its head sloped, and its muscles were so big that it didn't have a neck. Its nose spread across its face, and I could see the nostrils flaring and the pink inside. His mouth was huge and stretched from one side of its massive jaw to the other, and the lips were like a horse."

I was on the edge of my seat, listening. I whispered, "Sasquatch" under my breath.

Sam heard me.

"Yes, but at that time, I had never heard of Bigfoot or Sasquatch or anything like that. Other than a few old stories about monsters in the woods, I had no idea. I'm not sure how long we stood there facing each other before I realized why. It dawned on me that I was carrying its dinner. I nodded at the deer on my shoulders, then slid it down to the ground, and slowly backed away. When I was far enough away, it walked over to the deer, picked it up in one hand, then stepped into the woods and disappeared. It never took its eyes off me."

"What did you do next?" I asked, unable to hold back.

We heard the coyotes start up again, but they sounded much farther away this time. Sam cocked his head as if to listen to their mournful cries. His head dipped again, and he stared into the flames.

"I sank to my knees...and cried," he confessed. "I'm not ashamed. But I cried. I cried like a baby. Fear is a *powerful* emotion. It has a way of bringing out your deepest feelings. It was overpowering. It was not because of the creature, but about the war and the things I saw there, the things I did that I didn't want to do. It all came crashing down on me. I remembered everything- from the time I got on the plane, being dropped from a Huey in the middle of a firefight- seeing my buddies die. Missing home, everything. I could see their faces. I remembered how scared I was when I was there and how thankful I was to make it back home," he said.

He sat there a moment and collected his thoughts before continuing.

"My mind was numb to it all, and after a while, I stopped knowing anyone. Oh, I knew their names, but I would never let myself know them closely because I knew that I would probably lose them. I didn't want to carry that. I felt guilty for that. Like I had dishonored them by not getting to know them."

Sam paused again. I didn't want to push him, so I sat quietly.

"I guess I must've sat there in the snow for several minutes before I picked myself up and hiked back to camp. I was drained. No energy left. But I felt like there was nothing left inside weighing on me. Like a burden was lifted from me. Relieved. I built my fire back up and just sat there. I wasn't thinking. I suppose I was scared when I first saw the monster, but that passed quickly. After it left with the deer, I wasn't afraid. Not anymore. I never got the sense that I should be. I only got a sense that I had interrupted his hunt and that I owed him. And I knew it was a *him*. No mistaking that."

"Did you pack up and get the heck out?" I asked.

"Not right away. I stayed another night. As I said, I wasn't scared. I was at peace. I think, somehow, the creature helped me find the healing that I needed. And to be honest, I wasn't sure if what I had witnessed was real or not. I had a lot of self-doubts. I thought I was going through something that I couldn't explain- visions or something. I didn't know, but I wasn't afraid.

"The following day, I packed up and started the hike out. By nightfall, I had made it to the river and found my boat. I threw my duffle in, laid my bow on top, and then slid it out into the water. The wind was blowing hard and whipping through the trees blowing snow everywhere. The water was white-capping, very choppy, and I had to try to paddle against the current. I knew this wasn't going to be a fun trip. I pulled my boat back to me with the rope and started to step in when I lost my balance on the icy bank and slid into the water. *Then*, I was scared."

"Holy hell, what'd you do?"

"I struggled to get back on the bank. I couldn't get a

handhold on anything, and the current was too strong. The boat took off down the river, and I didn't have a chance to grab onto it. Not that I could've anyway. I just knew for sure I was a goner. The water was too cold, and I didn't have the strength left. I let go and felt myself float away with the current. I remember thinking that was my favorite bow. I had carved an eagle into the riser– my best work. It's funny what goes through a person's mind when facing death. A feeling of peace came over me, and I stopped shaking. I had no regrets. I had a good life. I only felt sorry for my mother, who would never know what happened to her son."

Sam suddenly scrambled to his feet and danced next to the fire again. He sang a few words. I didn't understand, but maybe he was giving praise. When he finished, he sat back down. I was dying to ask more questions, but I didn't dare speak.

"The great spirit was taking me, and I just let go, with everything, mind – spirit – body. I just let go."

Sam stopped and caught his breath. His sudden burst of energy had zapped his strength, or it seemed like it did. But a moment later, he continued.

"I woke up next to a roaring fire. I had no idea how I got there or even how long I had been there. It was daytime, and that's about all I knew. My clothes were dry, so it had to be hours anyway. I looked around, confused. Everything was like a whirlwind in my head. I didn't recognize where I was. Not right away.

"I guess I hadn't eaten anything in a while - just some coffee is all I remembered having. Maybe I wasn't right in the head because of it; I don't know. When I stood and looked around the camp, I smelled something. I wasn't sure what it was, but it smelled good. Then I saw what it was. In the fire, I saw the tail of a fish sticking out from between two planks of wood that were tied together with string or vine or something. I didn't question it. Not once. I ripped it out of the fire and ate like a starving man. It was the best meal I had ever eaten. It was so good," he laughed.

"After I ate, I looked around the area. What I found was-interesting. There were three long branches on the ground near the fire."

Sam used the stick he was poking the fire with and drew the shape out on the ground. "Kind of like a capital letter 'T' that had an extra cross on it. In the bottom outside of the T was a stack of three rocks. And, there were enormous footprints all around. Twice as big as mine and barefoot."

Sam had my attention now!

"I've heard of this kind of thing before," I said. "The sticks and rocks, I mean."

"At the time, I had no idea what it meant. I don't think it was meant for me."

"What do you think it meant? You think it was a message to others that may find you or something?" I asked.

"Yes, I think it left it so that others that may come upon me knew that I was to be left alone. Maybe it meant friend. I didn't know and still don't, but I was grateful."

I felt he didn't mind me talking and asking questions. I could read the sign when the time came that he was annoyed with me or didn't want to be disturbed when he was speaking. He wasn't giving me any indication of that, not yet anyway.

"So, what happened then?" I asked.

"When I looked around a little more, I discovered that I was in a familiar place and not too far off the trail. Only steps from the river. And on the right side. Even though it had been four or five years since I had been there, it all came back to me like riding a bike. Someone or something dragged my boat up on the bank. My pack was right where I had left it, but my bow and quiver of arrows were gone."

"You think the Squatch took it?"

"Of that, I have no doubt. I think it was a trade for my life and one I'd gladly do again. I think he got *took* on the deal," he laughed. "But it was my best bow, after all. After I ate my fill, I grabbed my duffle and hiked home. It took me the rest of the day. I finally walked into the house just as it got dark. My mother asked, 'No deer?' I just shrugged my shoulders but said nothing. She had to see that I no longer carried my bow but said nothing. Maybe she knew."

"Did you ever see it again?" I asked. "The Bigfoot, I mean."

"I hunted every year since then, hiked all over these mountains. Never seen it again or any sign that what happened was real. I never got the feeling of being afraid, and sometimes I felt that I wasn't alone. Maybe it was the creator's way of cleansing me. Spiritual healing."

***

Sam was tired. I helped him back to the house and made sure he was comfortable. I went back outside and put the fire out before turning in. I couldn't sleep that night. I lay awake thinking about my friend's story. I had no reason to disbelieve him.

Sam permitted me to invite a friend to do some camping with me and explore the area of his encounter.

I have camped, hunted, and ridden four-wheelers for many years all over those mountains where Sam grew up. The Kiamichi's are full of wildlife- gray foxes, coyotes, bobcats, turkeys, bears, and even mountain lions. Fish are plentiful in the creeks and rivers. There have also been many reported sightings of Bigfoot. Though I have combed those mountains, crisscrossing ridges, hunting deer, and fishing those backwater creeks and ponds, I've never actually seen a

Sasquatch. I did have a bit of a scare late one evening.

I learned that Sam had passed away not long ago, which brought a considerable amount of sadness to me. I did talk to his eldest son, Richard, on the phone when Sam passed. It was a brief conversation but one very profound.

Richard said, "Dad spoke of you often, said you were a good friend. He would want you to know of his passing, but we just now came across your number. He wanted to leave you something to remember him by."

I think I said something like, "I'm very sorry to hear that. I considered Sam a good friend too and will miss him. My deepest condolences. But what do you mean, he left me something?"

I was curious about that. I knew Sam wasn't a wealthy man and didn't have much of anything. I was shocked and more than a bit confused, consumed with sadness. I didn't know what to think.

Richard said, "It's a bow. Dad was known as a good bow maker, but this one I don't recognize. It's old and looks like it's seen better days. Probably not worth much other than to dad, but he wanted you to have it. It has an eagle carved into it. I wouldn't suggest stringing it up, though. It could break."

Richard continued, "When Dad was sick, the hospice worker said it was on the front porch leaning against the door one morning when she got here. When I asked him about it, he said an old friend he had gifted it to must have brought it back to him in the night. He never said who," Richard said. "That's when he said that he wanted you to have it, said you'd know why."

I hung the bow on the wall in my office. Every time I look at it, I'm reminded of my friend, Sam, his stories, and the bonds of friendship - in all its forms.

5

HUNTERS CHASED OUT OF THE WOODS

Witness: *Jack Edwards*
Interviewed: *July 18, 2018*
Location: *Eufaula, Alabama - 5:13 p.m.*

When I traveled through the south, I kept hearing about a guy named Jack who claimed that he and his buddies were run out of the woods by several creatures while hunting in Colorado. It took some doing to track him down, but I finally found him through a friend of a friend. I called him, and we were able to set up a meeting.

I met with Jack late one evening in a small diner near Lake Eufaula. It was one of those places where the locals hung out. Not many people traveling through would stop in. Not that it was hidden or run-down, just that it was a small, old-fashioned mom-and-pop type place. Old-timers and farmers would come in and linger all morning, drinking coffee, telling lies, and swapping stories. Most people would pass it by for one of the nicer franchises up the road.

I arrived about fifteen minutes early and found a booth in the back corner. I ordered a cup of coffee as I waited for Jack to arrive. I had just set out my recorder and notepad when I saw a tall, broad-shouldered man approach. He reached out with his hand and introduced himself as Jack. He recognized the clothes I told him I would be wearing. I stood and shook hands and asked him to have a seat.

We ordered a couple of bacon cheeseburgers, and while we ate, we got to know each other with talk about hunting and fishing. I didn't want to push too hard to get his story. I figured we had plenty of time, and he would open up easier on his own. We skimmed the basics when I first called, but we didn't go into many details. He said he didn't want me to think he was crazy, but I assured him that wouldn't be the case. I've heard it all before.

"Most people give me a hard time about it and don't believe me, but it's all true. I think I stumbled on to where they live, and they ran me the hell out of there," Jack said.

I've heard many stories where the creatures have scared people away, but I just said, "Really?"

"Damn right," Jack continued. "It happened a while back when I went on a hunting trip with a couple of buddies in Colorado. I'd never been hunting up there for mule deer but always wanted to. We were way back in the mountains. Places normal people don't go on any kind of regular basis. But yeah. I thought they were going to kill me, and no one would ever find my body. I'll never go back again. Not there anyway. It was like they were stalking me or something, reminded me of that movie, Jurassic Park- where the Velociraptors surrounded the hunter in the jungle and attacked him from all sides." He paused and looked down into his cup, then slowly raised his eyes to meet mine. "I bet you already think I'm crazy, don't you?"

"I don't know you well enough to make a judgment call like that," I said, "but I'd sure like to hear about it."

I have to say; I was intrigued. I didn't know Jack from Adam, but I knew I needed to hear his story before concluding anything. Anything to do with Bigfoot has always been like a magnet for me. The stories draw me in like a moth to a flame, and Jack's statement that he had found their home was a bonfire.

Most of the time, I let folks tell their story without interrupting them. I make notes along the way, and when they finish, I ask lots of questions. I'll ask the same questions over and over in different ways. I find that when I do, I can poke holes in the story. If they're lying or unsure, I'll know by the way they answer. I have no tolerance for lies and hoaxes. I grew up hunting everything from squirrels and rabbits to deer and elk. I know a thing or two about the outdoors. I've been interested in anything to do with the subject of Sasquatch since the '70s. Whether one believes or not makes little difference in how entertaining the account is.

Jack got very quiet and looked me square in the eyes. I suppose he was sizing me up, trying to decide if he could trust me or not. He leaned forward and began.

(As told in his words, edited only for clarity)

"It was back in 2002 when it happened. It took us a couple of days to make the trip. We traveled out there in a Suburban pulling a sixteen-foot flatbed trailer with three four-wheelers and several large coolers for the meat."

I nodded. "Typical setup."

"Exactly. Nothing out of the ordinary. My buddies had gotten a hunting lease that had recently come open. They had a spot for one more hunter, and I got lucky, or so I thought when they asked me to come. It was all primitive camping, though, no cabin or anything. Being so far away, of course, we weren't able to go scout it beforehand.

"We stopped at a little town for final supplies and were planning to stay for a week or so.

"It wasn't difficult to find. We found the gate, and the combination lock opened with the code we were given, so we knew we were at the right place. We drove back into a place that the owner told us to look for, the best place to set up camp. There was a clearing with a fire ring built with rocks that others had used before. We got out, got the tent set up, and still had time to do a little scouting before it got too dark. Everything went fine that following day. Not much to talk about. The weather was great. Not too cold, and the wind was consistent, making it just right for hunting.

"Well, we had been at camp for a couple of days, and none of us hadn't seen much. No shooters* anyway," Jack said. He took a sip of his coffee before continuing.

"I decided that I needed to go deeper, maybe cross the river and get back into the places that only a billy goat would go. I had spotted an area the first day where I thought I may be able to cross."

Jack pushed his ball cap back and stared out the window a moment. Perhaps remembering details of the event. I never got the impression that he was making anything up.

"Early the next day, I got up before my two buddies, packed my stuff, put my tree stand on my back, and headed off on my own. I left them sleeping. I followed an old game trail a couple of miles back until I found a shallow place to cross the river. I had to scramble a little on the other side getting out because it was a little steeper over there and slippery, but it wasn't too hard. Keep in mind that it was still dark, and I was only using my flashlight to get around. With snow on the ground, I wasn't worried about getting lost.

"The sky turned a little grayer, and I figured I had less than half an hour before sunrise. I wouldn't have known if I hadn't stopped to rest. I turned my flashlight off and looked up through the trees- the only way to see. I wanted to find a tree that I could climb to give me a good view of any game trails that might lead down to the river. I guess I hadn't figured the terrain was as rough as it was, though. I'll tell you, I was huffing and puffing," Jack chuckled a little and took another drink of his coffee.

I knew he was forty-eight years old from our previous phone conversation. He was in his early thirties when his encounter took place. Jack was still in good shape, a little over six feet tall, weighing probably two hundred twenty pounds. He worked in a sawmill and looked well able to handle himself.

"Anyway, when I saw the gray in the sky, I knew the sun wouldn't be far behind. I wanted to find a good spot before that happened. So, I picked up the pace a little bit.

A few minutes later, I heard footsteps just off the trail in the thicker brush just beyond where I could see. I stopped to listen, but when I did, the footsteps stopped. But as soon as I took off again, the footsteps did too. Whoever or whatever it was, paralleled me maybe fifteen yards away in the brush.

"Now I've been in the woods all my life, and I know what two feet compared to four feet sounds like when they're walking, and this was definitely two feet. I would walk a few steps, and it would walk a few steps. If I stopped, it stopped. So a thousand things start going through my mind now. Did one of my buddies follow me out here and is messing with me? Or is there somebody else out there hunting, and we don't know about it? If that's the case, why haven't they said something? Is this other idiot going to shoot me thinking I'm a deer? If this other hunter has no clue that I'm a person, he might think he's stalking a deer and shoot!"

He stopped to take another sip. He finished the cup and motioned for the waitress to bring him another. I sipped my coffee and kept recording, still not wanting to interrupt with questions. I didn't want to cause him to lose his thoughts. I needed him to recall everything as it happened.

"I don't know. It had me a little jumpy. I'll tell you that. So I decided that I would go ahead and shine my flashlight over there and call out. It's better to ruin a hunt than to get shot," he laughed nervously. "I shined my light over there and called out. Not loud, just loud enough to be heard from that distance. I said, 'Hey, are you a hunter?' But I didn't get a response. I tried again and still nothing, so I stood there for a few minutes, kept shining my light around, never heard anything. Finally, I took off walking and didn't get more than three steps when I heard it walking again. I pulled up short and spun around with my light. Whatever it was took off running away - crunch crunch, crunch, crunch– faster and faster away from me. Then it was gone.

"Whoever or whatever it was, was gone. So then I was really freaked out because I knew for a fact that whatever that was, whoever that was, was most definitely on two feet. By now, the sun was up. That made me feel a little better. Of course, it was still kind of dark in the woods, but I could see well enough that I didn't need my light.

"I heard the river gurgling. It was still on my left, not too far off, less than fifty yards from this game trail I was following. But another trail intersected the one I was on, and it looked like it came down from the ridge leading to the river. I decided to turn up and find a good spot that overlooked where these two came together. Both trails seemed very used, and I'd already seen several deer tracks, and some were pretty good size.

"I found a tall sycamore tree that would give me a good position, and I could get pretty high up it because it didn't have any low hanging limbs. I set my things down and got my treestand around the trunk, and got ready to climb. I had to saw off a few small limbs, but they were small and didn't slow me down. I climbed nearly thirty feet up before stopping. And before you ask – yes, I know for a fact it was 30 feet because that's how long my rope is that I use to pull my rifle and pack up with."

The waitress came by and topped off our coffee. Jack thanked her and got up to use the bathroom. I took the opportunity to make a few notes for questions later concerning weather conditions, timeline, clothing worn, and any types of scents or sprays that he may have been using.

Jack returned a few minutes later, took a drink, and launched into his story again.

"Sorry about that," Jack said. "Where was I? Oh yeah. I had settled in my stand. I carry a small screw-in hook that I can tap into the tree and hang my pack on. Once I had that secured and my rifle hauled up, I settled in and got comfortable. I figured to be there 'til dark unless I got a good one, of course. This is Colorado, so there's snow on the ground, and it's cold, but the trails weren't bad at all. Just perfect for spot and stalk, easy tracking.

"I guess I had been in my stand for a good hour when I heard something hit the tree I was in, felt it too. It was a solid thump like a rock or something. I didn't move. I just shifted my eyes and scanned the area that I could see. At first, I thought it could have been a woodpecker or something. You know how you start trying to imagine what it could have been, given the circumstances."

I nodded, "Yeah, I know what you're talking about."

"Yeah, so, I thought it might be a woodpecker, squirrel, broken limb- just about anything- but I was perfectly comfortable, wasn't cold, and wasn't thinking about whatever that was earlier. I had forgotten all about that, just concentrated on looking for deer. I wasn't about to move. Even though I was sitting thirty feet above the ground, deer can spot things if it moves. The art of camouflage is movement, or the lack of, really. Just don't move. Concealment and visual deception means blending into your environment."

I agreed. I've taken more than my share of deer in the field, and camo is important, but he's right. There are thousands of trees, plants, rocks, and animals in the forest, lots of things for the mind to take in and process. Most animals have a fright and flight survival instinct. They are attuned to their environment and can spot things that don't belong, but they may not react to it unless it moves.

"A few minutes went by. I never moved, not a single muscle, but I kept my eyes moving, scanning every part of the woods I could see. I was listening, concentrating hard, but I didn't see anything, nothing new. Then I heard this loud thump answered by another one coming from my left, which is the trail I had just come down. Now I've been in the woods hunting all my life. I don't remember a time when I wasn't. When you sit in a tree stand for hours from daylight to dusk, you see and hear all kinds of things. Natural things. Limbs break. Trees fall. It's all-natural. You can tell, but in this case, this was a knock followed by another knock 50 yards away, not tree breaks or limbs, so again my eyes are moving everywhere. I'm not moving a muscle because, once again, the art of deception and disguise is controlling your movement. Snipers practice long crawls for hours and hours, sometimes without moving. This is the same sort of thing when you're deer hunting. Don't move, and the chances of being spotted in the woods are much lower. I was wearing camouflage, obviously from head to toe. It was just a simple snow pattern, and against the bark of the sycamore tree, I felt pretty comfortable sitting 30 feet above the ground, just below several limbs. But I was getting a little freaked out. I thought that whatever that was that I heard walking through the woods this morning must live in this area, and that really got my heart racing.

"But I had the comfort of knowing that I have a .300 Win Mag with me, not to mention a 357 Magnum on my hip that I always carried in woods where there might be bears or big cats. Just something I've always done. It gives me peace of mind, I suppose.

"A few minutes later, I heard another wood knock, but that time it was much further away and to my right, just the one knock. I thought, okay, whatever it is, it's getting further away. I'm good. But then I heard two more knocks, one to my left and one directly in front of me. One of them sounded pretty close, but they were moving around. Whatever is out there, there are at least three of them. And that really put me on edge. I was frozen, scared stiff, not moving a muscle, spine-tingling, nerves shot to hell.

"I had on gloves holding my rifle across the braces of my stand. My thumb rested on the safety, and my finger ran just along the edge of the stock. I had one in the chamber and three rounds in the mag. I also had sixteen other rounds in my pack, six rounds in the .357, and a speed load round in my bag, so I figured I was pretty good as far as ammo goes. But I got to tell you. A thousand things start running through your head. But right then, the only thing that I could think was, those are Bigfoot, and they're hunting me.

"I've heard all the stories, you know? The wood knocks, the pine cones, and rocks thrown at campers. All those sorts of things. So, now I'm thinking, if that's what this is, would I shoot one? Could I shoot one? I mean, I don't know. I've never seen one and have no idea what I would do, so I started running through the scenarios. By my count, there are three of them out there, and it seemed like they were signaling each other. Do they know where I am? Did they lose me? Did the one that was trailing me lose me, and they're communicating, looking for me, searching? I didn't have any way of knowing. So the next question was, how the hell do I get out of there? Do I wait until it gets dark? From everything I've heard, they see better in the dark than they do in the daylight. I don't know, who the hell knows? Do you know what I mean?"

I nodded and said, "Yeah, I know exactly what you're saying."

He continued, "So I'm trying to figure out what to do next. I'm nervous as hell. Shaking, feeling the cold, but I don't think it was the weather that caused that. I needed to get down, but there were thirty feet straight between me and the ground. How do I do that without being seen? But then again, I don't know if they know where I am or not. To be honest with you, I was pretty scared because I've never been in a situation like that, ever. Who would ever think they would be in a position like that? I felt myself starting to sweat on my forehead. I needed to wipe it away before it fell into my eye, but I hated to move. I waited as long as I could, but finally, I just couldn't take it anymore. It's more annoying than a fly or mosquito buzzing. I slowly reached up, and just as I touched my forehead, the bushes exploded in front of me, not more than fifty yards away.

"My god, I thought I was going to have a heart attack right then and there. So, my question about if they knew where I was or not just got answered. I just gave my position away. This *thing*, I don't know what it was, was apparently stalking me. It probably had an idea of where I was but didn't know exactly. Not until I moved and gave my position away.

"All I saw was this brush pile covered with snow explode

like a grenade just went off or something. I never saw what caused it but heard these fast, heavy thuds and limbs snapping and something crash through the woods on the other side of the little ridge. It must have run at least fifty yards away from me, then almost in a complete circle in seconds, and then I heard nothing. That's when I knew I needed to get the hell out of there.

"But here's the problem - I needed to let down my pack and my rifle first before I could start climbing down. Those climbing tree stands are not fast even though they're pretty simple to operate, and I had my safety harness on, which slows you down even more. I thought, okay, I could unbuckle my harness and climb down as fast as I could. When I got close, I could hang off the platform and jump the rest of the way. But what happens if I break my damn leg or sprain an ankle or any number of other things? I froze. I don't think I moved, but it felt like I had already run a marathon. My heart was pounding so hard. I was just waiting because I was thirty feet up in the air. I don't care if this thing is 10 ft tall. It can't reach *me* before *I* can get it with my 300 Win Mag. But, there are at least two, possibly three.

"I started going over options in my head. Option one, and my safest bet, is to stay put and wait for these things to go away. I've got food, but I could end up being out here all night and freeze to death. Okay, not the best option. Option two, lower down my pack and my rifle, take the time to climb down, then shag-ass out of there. After another fifteen minutes of trying option one, I decided, nope. Option two it is!"

He laughed at that last statement and took a sip of his coffee.

"I lowered my pack down with my rifle. I didn't hear anything or see anything during that process, so I turned around in my stand, got my feet in the hooks, and started climbing down. I got a few feet, then lowered my safety harness and repeated the process. I got down maybe halfway when I heard something crash in the woods again. I couldn't tell where it came from because, to be honest, my heart was pounding so hard I thought it was going to beat out of my chest. I'm still a good fifteen feet up, but I figured, screw it. I unsnapped my safety harness, took it off the tree, and dropped it to the ground. I climbed down until I was maybe five feet off the ground then jumped.

"I picked up my rifle first and took a look around. Nothing. I grabbed my pack and threw it on my shoulder. I just left my harness there, and my tree stand attached to the tree, and I took off down the trail. Slowly, at first, because I was looking around everywhere with my rifle at the ready. I had gone maybe fifty feet when I heard another tree knock. It couldn't have been ten ft away. I spun and looked in that direction but didn't see anything. I remember thinking at the time that sometimes you can be looking right at something and not see it- look right over it. Then another knock came from the other side. It was a little further away, and I spun around, but I didn't see anything there either. I started moving again, walking, slow and steady, keeping my rifle ready in front of me and my eyes looking everywhere.

"Suddenly, I heard footsteps again, really close to me, on my right side, but it sounded like they were running away from me. It was out of earshot in a matter of seconds. I never saw what it was, but I felt a little relieved.

"I knew I needed to get the hell out of there, man. These things, whatever they are, seemed to be hunting me. I was in pretty damn good shape, and I could run, but I knew it would be tough going because of the snow and ice. Whether or not I could keep my footing while running in that terrain was the question. But I didn't give a damn. I took off. A couple of times, I damn near went down. Carrying a backpack and a rifle in your hand, it's nothing more than reckless abandon. I just knew I was going to bite it and go rolling. If that happened, they could be on me in seconds. Then I would be done for.

Jack stopped, sat back, and let out a long breath. He gulped his coffee and stared out the window. Neither of us spoke. I didn't want to interrupt his thoughts, so I just waited. He seemed to collect himself and picked up where he left off.

"Luckily, that didn't happen. I got to this turn in the trail that goes alongside the river again. I slowed down a little because I couldn't see around that curve. I thought, damn, what a perfect place for an ambush. But there was nothing I could do about it now. I was committed. Committed to a head-first collision course with whatever's around that bend. I came to a skidding stop right at the corner, slowing down just enough to make sure that I didn't lose my feet. I kind of banged up against a tree, and when I did, I shook the whole tree knocking snow and ice off the limbs, and dumped it all right on top of me. I waited a few seconds and caught my breath before taking off again.

"I could see the trail as it paralleled along the riverbank, but there was nothing there. I stopped and listened every few feet, but I wasn't seeing or hearing anything else. I forced myself to breathe and calm down. I think I was able to gather my damn wits about me then. I looked down, and I saw this track in the snow going across the trail. It was fresh, and I'll tell you when I saw it, I knew, I *knew*- what the hell it was. That track had to be every bit of eighteen inches long, and it looked like a giant human footprint. When I saw it, I stopped to take it in for a second, and I remember goosebumps started crawling all over my body. Maybe that's how animals feel when they're being hunted, I don't know.

"I felt like they were stalking me and were just playing with me like a rat in a maze. As fast as they seemed to move, they could have me at any time. I pulled my rifle up and made sure my thumb was on the safety, ready to fire, to reassure myself. I looked around. My head was on a swivel, jumping at every little sound, continuously searching but didn't see or hear anything. I started walking again, just a few steps down the trail and heard a couple of wood knocks to my right. Like boom boom boom, and then there was a reply from my left, boom boom boom. The ones on my right were a little behind me, and as I said, the river was on my right, maybe fifty feet or so. Whatever it was, was between me and the river, but where did the third one go?"

"How did you know they were wood knocks? I mean, was it obvious? Have you heard that sound before?"

"Oh, yeah. Very obvious. It sounded like a Louisville slugger in the hands of Paul Bunyon. I mean, it echoed out there in those woods like explosions. That'll set your nerves on fire. I damn sure didn't notice the cold anymore. I know it's hard to explain, but it was terrifying to think about the things that were doing that."

"No, I get it. I know what you mean," I assured him.

"As I said, I'm good in the woods, a pretty good tracker, so I'm not going to get lost. Especially following my own tracks in the snow," he laughed. "I saw my trail from earlier, so I was comfortable knowing where I was going. That was never in question. The question was, am I going in the direction that *I* wanted to go or the direction that *they* wanted me to go?

"I know they weren't humans. No human could move like that, not out there on that terrain. All I could think about was getting out of there alive. Sure, I had a rifle with me, but you can't shoot what you can't see. Hell, even if I did see it, I'm not sure that I could have shot one if that's what it was.

"I guess I was probably a couple of miles away from our

campsite. If I took off running, I could probably get to the crossing in about ten or fifteen minutes and then another twenty or so to camp. I'm not sure why I thought I'd be any safer at the campsite, other than that we had a vehicle. I sure was wishing I had one of the quads with me," he laughed.

"But what the hell. I took off jogging. I can't call what I was doing running because there was just no way I could. Not with insulated bibs, coat, boots, a pack, and a rifle. It was probably more of a balanced wobble," he laughed. "I'm sure I looked a sight.

"I had my focus ahead of me the whole time but kept my eyes moving constantly. I caught a glimpse of one of them. It was brief, but I made it out to be about thirty yards out, staying in a brush line even with me. It was just a flash in the brush. I picked the pace up. I was in good shape, never smoked or anything, but my adrenaline was pumping so hard and pounding in my ears that I started getting tunnel vision. All I could seem to make out were the few feet in front of me as I stumbled along. Again, I didn't even think about stopping and taking a shot. If it came to that, I wanted to be damn sure of what I was shooting.

"I guess I ran for several minutes before I finally slowed down. My legs felt like rubber. I was hoping they had stopped chasing me. I was breathing hard, panting like a dog, doubled over trying to get my wits about me when I heard a *whoop*. That's all I can describe it as, a whoop - just one. I couldn't tell where it came from, but I jerked up and looked everywhere. I probably looked like an old tom turkey, bobbing around. I could hear the gurgling of the water nearby. I was still on the trail, but I noticed that I wasn't following my tracks anymore. I must've passed the spot where I crossed the river that morning. I turned and looked back down the trail. That's when I saw the other one.

You're not going to believe this, but I swear it's true.

When I turned, this *thing*, that's the only thing I know to call it, jumped from one side of the trail to the other in a single jump. I heard a couple of heavy footsteps before it jumped, and then it cleared at least twenty feet, easy, about three feet off the ground. I saw it for only a split second, but I swear, the way it jumped, it looked like a giant orangutan. Its hair was orange. Not black, brown, or red like you hear, but orange. Bright orange, I kid you not. Its arms were just as long as its legs, and it was huge, just massive. It landed on the other side, went down on all fours, and disappeared. With that kind of speed, I knew I didn't have a chance in hell of outrunning it. If it wanted me, it could have had me at any time. It was as quiet as a deer and something that big should have been like a bull in a china closet busting through the bushes and trees, but it wasn't. It was like a ghost. That made me realize that every time I heard one, it was only because it *wanted* me to hear it. I didn't see its face, just its side. It didn't have a snout like a bear, though, just a flat face. Its face and hands were the only things that didn't have any hair. But its hair was long and course-looking.

"I threw my rifle up to my shoulder and tried to scope it, but I couldn't see anything from my lower position on the trail. I listened hard, really hard, and I thought I heard someone talking. Only it wasn't talking, not really. It was more like a couple of pissed-off bobcats. I don't know how to explain it exactly."

"Are you familiar with the Sierra Sounds?" I asked him.

He shook his head no and said, "I don't guess so."

"I'll explain later. Please go on."

He cleared his throat and continued with his recounting.

"When I heard that, I tried really hard to make it out, but as I said, it just wasn't any kind of *language*. But they were communicating. Of that much, I'm sure.

I knew I wasn't going to sneak out of there, and I wasn't

sure how far past my old trail I was. I had no choice but to keep going because I damn sure wasn't going back the way I just came. I would just have to look for another place to cross.

"I guess I walked at least another half an hour when I came to a spot right next to the river. The trail dipped through a small clump of saplings near the water's edge. I couldn't believe how lucky I was. The water ran over the top of these granite slabs in that spot, and it was easy to walk across. You better believe that I scrambled my butt across, hit that trail on the other side, and shagged ass back to camp.

"I glimpsed one of the mountain peaks through the trees, and that gave me my bearing. I kept looking back to make sure they weren't following me. At one point, I could have sworn I saw one standing at the edge of the river, but when I brought my scope up to get a better look, it was gone.

"I got back to the camp, and the first thing I did was check my ammo. Here's the weirdest part about all this. What time do you think it is now?"

I guess I must have had a puzzled look.

"I mean, judging from when I left that morning in the dark to the time I got back to the camp?"

"Oh, I see. I would think it would be around mid-morning, no later than noon," I said.

"Yeah, me too. But when I walked into camp, I had to use my flashlight. That's when it dawned on me. It was almost dark. Ten minutes later, I saw a flashlight flickering around. It was one of my buddies coming back to camp. Somehow, several hours had passed. It was the weirdest feeling. I lost several hours. Now you tell me, how does that happen?"

Jack seemed earnest in the recounting of his story. At no point did I get an indication that he was making any part of it up, and I had no reason to doubt his encounter.

"What happened when your buddy got back? Did you tell

him what happened?"

"Well, he came into camp and asked me if I had seen anything, meaning any deer, of course. He put his stuff down, and I think that's when he noticed the ashen look on my face. He said that it looked like I had seen a ghost. All of the color had drained out of me. Our other buddy got back to camp just as I had finished telling Phil about what happened, so I had to tell my story again."

"Did they believe you?" I asked.

"I think they were skeptical at first and kept asking me if I was just messing with them, but as the night wore on, I think I convinced them, especially when I told them that I wasn't going back out there and was ready to leave."

"I bet," I said. "I guess they believed you then? Did you pack up and leave, or did you stay?"

"We ended up staying the night. They weren't about to flush this trip down the drain that quickly. Besides, it was too late to try and pack up the camp. They both agreed to go with me the next day to find my stand and bring it back. I told them I wasn't going back across the river alone.

"That night, we built a fire up and slept with our guns within reach. Our tent was one of those thick, heavy canvas ones that looked like a small cabin. We had our cots and a wood stove inside. We brought cut firewood just for it and kept a fire in it too. It kept that tent warm and comfortable, but we made sure the fire outside was burning all night. We had gathered plenty of dead wood for it."

"Did anything happen through the night?" I asked.

"No, nothing happened, but we hardly got any sleep. The next day, I don't think any of us was eager to get started. We finally rousted out of bed after sunup and fixed some coffee and a little something to eat. We decided that we would backtrack across the river, find my stand, and, if we had enough time, hunt that evening on *this* side when we got back. It shouldn't take that long to hike in a couple of miles and retrieve it. We loaded up with all the ammo we could carry and set out.

"It didn't take long to find my trail. We were at the river crossing in probably about half an hour. When we got to the other side, I think that's when they started believing me. There were tracks all over the place. Huge bare footprints. These things were enormous. Even if I was trying to fool them, there's no way that I could have made that many fake prints. But here's the funny thing. We wanted to track them into the brush, but every time we followed a trail, they disappeared."

"As in just stopped altogether?"

"Exactly," Jack said.

"Were the woods pretty dense? In other words, do you think they could have been traveling through the trees?"

"Yeah, and that's exactly what we thought too. That made us even more freaked out. So now, not only were we watching the ground, looking behind every tree and bush, but now we're breaking our necks to keep an eye on the damn trees."

"Yeah, that must have been an eerie feeling."

"We gave up trying to track these things. I mean, what the hell were we going to do if we found one anyway? It's not like we were going to shoot one and bring it back. I think we only followed the tracks a short distance just to make sure they weren't still around or something. I don't know. But we got back on my trail and followed it around to my tree stand. We might as well stayed at camp.

"My stand was one of those climbers and built solid, brand new. It attaches around the tree and secures with a cable. It was still attached to the tree, maybe four feet off the ground, when I left it behind. I had slid out of my harness and jumped to the ground. We found the base of my stand still attached to the tree, but it was bent to hell. The top section had been ripped off the tree and thrown in the bushes. My harness was nowhere to be found."

"Are you serious?"

"Oh yeah. The tree was torn to hell, too, from where these things tried to rip it off. That took some strength."

"So, what happened then?"

"That's when we got the hell out of Dodge," Jack said with a slight laugh. "We weren't sticking around any longer. We had the camp packed up before nightfall."

"Did you go home?" I asked.

"No, actually, we went to a little town a few hours away and got a room that night. I think we felt a lot better once we were clear of that area. The further away, the better. The next day, we had breakfast at a little café and made a plan to go back, only to a different area. Our lease was a little over three hundred acres, with most of it on the near side of the river. I think we just needed the time to get our heads on and think about it. Once we were away from there, I think we got our courage back. We didn't see or hear anything else for the rest of the trip. We damn sure didn't cross that river, though. We all tagged out by the last day, but we never told anyone else about it while we were there."

"Let's go back to the sounds you heard when you thought they were talking. I mentioned the Sierra Sounds. These sounds were recorded by Ron Morehead several years ago and are thought to be a type of language these creatures use to communicate. Let me play a snippet of it and tell me if this is anything like what you heard."

I pulled a YouTube video up and played the sounds. Jack's face drained of any color.

"Yes!" he said, "That's very damn close to what I heard. It wasn't that fast, but it was garbled. I couldn't make heads or tails of it, but that's it."

*Shooters - a buck with a large rack. In many cases, hunters are allowed only one buck and don't want to spoil their hunt by shooting the first one they see. They would rather wait for a large trophy size and save the little ones for the last day if they still haven't filled their tag.

6

HONOBIA CREEK BIGFOOT

Witness: *Personal Account*
Date of Encounter: *October 18, 2008*

The year was 2008. It was an early fall evening, and I was on Highway 59 South headed for Honobia Creek, Oklahoma, in the Kiamichi Mountains. That stretch of highway is one of the most scenic drives in the state. Every year thousands of people make the trip just for the fall foliage. I was headed out to meet up with a group of friends and spend the weekend riding four-wheelers over the mountain trails. I was coming from a different direction than the others, so I arrived before everyone else.

My buddy owned two cabins on one of the mountains just above the old Honobia Creek cabin store a few miles back. As you pass by the store and start going up the mountain, you have to slow down to find the old logging road leading back to the cabins. It's a hidden road. Not on purpose. It's just hard to find unless you know what you're looking for. The road winds around in and out of trees, with switchback-hairpin turns over ruts and stumps. It's rugged.

I drove a four-wheel-drive truck with a flatbed trailer hauling three four-wheelers. I had to take my time to get through there. It was dark by 10:00 p.m., with no moon or stars, so anything beyond the headlight beams was pitch black. The mountains made it seem darker still. I got to the first cabin, backed up, and got my trailer parked alongside the house when I realized I didn't have a key. I would have to wait on the rest of the guys to get there, and of course, there is no cell service.

I killed the engine, but my dash lights and radio remained on for about fifteen minutes before they went off automatically. I sat there listening to the radio until it finally turned off. When it did, it pitched me into inky darkness so black I literally could not see my hand in front of my face. To be honest, it was pretty spooky.

I sat there a few minutes when I started getting this uncomfortable, queasy feeling. I realize that you can be your own worst enemy in situations like that. Your mind can play tricks on you, and you can end up talking yourself into or out of some of those feelings. Possibly that's what I did. I reached into my console and pulled out my .45, and put it on my lap. You know, just in case. I had my windows down, and I could hear all the usual night sounds - crickets, cicadas, bullfrogs croaking. I mean, everything is alive in this pitch-black world.

I kicked back in my seat and started to relax a bit. Suddenly, a limb snapped, and I sat bolt right up in full alert. It came from over on my left side, just behind the cabin. I didn't have my flashlight out because it was stowed in my bag in the back seat somewhere, so I didn't even bother to reach for it. I still figured that the guys would be along any minute. It was probably just a raccoon, maybe a possum, no big deal. A few minutes later, I heard the crunch of dried leaves. The sound came from that same area. This time, *it didn't sound small.*

A million things ran through my head. I knew there were bears and mountain lions in those woods. We've seen hundreds of tracks before. Even though we're always at the cabins under the guise of Bigfoot hunting, we really used it as an excuse to go down there to ride four-wheelers, fish, and drink beer. I wasn't really worried about what I heard, and I felt pretty comfortable with my .45 on my lap. I know none of the guys were there yet because I would have seen their vehicles. There's nowhere else to park except in front of the cabin, so it's not them trying to scare me. I relaxed back into the seat and started thinking about the weekend. A few minutes later, I heard this *crunch* of two more steps. This time I'm positive they're steps and not a general rustling sound made by animals moving in the dried leaves.

I remember I had this weird feeling again. Very tense, almost agitated. I could feel my skin tingling like a slight jolt of electricity - a peculiar sense. That's when I noticed that it had gone silent. The crickets, cicadas, and bullfrogs - all stopped. Nothing. Nothing but deathly silence. Someone or something was there.

I heard another step, *crunch.* It sounded like it was just a few feet from my window, but I didn't have a flashlight to check it out, and I didn't want to turn on my headlights because as dark as it was when all the dash lights came on, they may blind *me.* I heard another *crunch* of leaves, and then I felt this- *presence-* right beside me, standing right by my door. It filled the entire window, looming over me in the darkness. The truck rocked ever so slightly. I knew something was there just inches away, and I guess I froze in fear. I'm sure I still had my .45 in my lap but never thought of using it.

The next thing I knew, I was parked at the Honobia store. I was breathing hard, trying to catch my breath, but I don't know how the hell I got out of there. It was like I had some kind of panic attack. My gun was lying in the seat beside me, the trailer with the four-wheelers still attached to my truck. Everything else was blank. I could *not* remember how the hell I got there. I suppose the fear was so overwhelming that my only reaction was to run.

I can't remember any time in my life that I was afraid to be in the woods. I have spent days alone on hunts, overnight camping. I don't get scared, especially if I'm carrying a gun. I'm not afraid of anything in the woods. I've never lost my sensibilities whatsoever, for any reason, but I still can't fathom what happened on that trip to Honobia Creek.

7

SLEEP PARALYSIS

Witness: *Gene Steele*
Interview Date: *May 22, 2019*
Location: *Tahlequah, Oklahoma*

(As told in his words, edited for clarity)

"In the summer of 2001, I came home late one night from a fishing trip. It was about 2 a.m., and, of course, my wife was in bed asleep, and the house was dark. When I checked the baby's room, I saw that he wasn't in his crib. I quietly looked in, and sure enough, he was in bed with momma. I didn't want to wake them, so I went to the guest room in the back of the house, showered, and went to bed.

"Our house had wooden floors with a crawlspace underneath. Though solid, when someone walked in one part of the house, another person could hear the footsteps on the other end if it were quiet inside.

"I had just laid down and pulled the covers up when I heard footsteps. I was facing the wall with my back to the open door. I thought maybe my wife had gotten up and was coming to check on me. Then the footsteps quickened into a run, bounding down the hallway and into my room. They were so fast that I didn't have time to react. In the next instant, something solid and heavy jumped on top of me, pinning me down. I was wide awake. The room was not completely dark as the yard light outside shined in through the window blinds, but I was frozen. I couldn't speak, couldn't move, couldn't breathe! Something held me down so hard that it felt like I was suffocating, but I couldn't see anyone there. I could see everything in the room, the dresser, the chest of drawers that stood at the end of the bed, the nightstand with the fan on top, but I couldn't any person or anything. This lasted for at least several seconds when just as suddenly as it came, it was gone. I could move again. As soon as it let go, I spun over, throwing the blanket off with my fist up, ready to hit someone, but no one was there. I was trembling, shaking from panic and anger. My heart was racing.

"I jumped out of bed, turned on the light, and immediately searched the entire house. My wife and son were sleeping peacefully, but I never heard or saw anyone."

*Sleep paralysis is a common condition identified by the medical industry as having a brief loss of muscle control after falling asleep or waking up. During this state, the victim may experience hallucinations.

Long ago, and before modern science discovered the causes of sleep paralysis, there were many contrived explanations for the phenomenon. One, in particular, was so prevalent that the occurrence is often referred to by name, the Old Hag Syndrome.

People thought that the feeling of intense pressure on one's chest was the physical manifestation of an evil spirit in the form of an old hag crushing its victim. There have been many reports of demonic visitations as well as alien abductions and out-of-body experiences during episodes.

8

UFO SIGHTED OVER STILWELL

Witness: *M. Jones*
Interviewed: *September 16, 2019*
Location of Occurrence: *Stilwell, Oklahoma - 6:30 p.m.*

(*As told in his words, edited for clarity*)

"Late one evening, my wife and I were driving home from being out shopping in Fort Smith. We stopped at a convenience store just west of Stilwell on Highway 100. It was winter because I remember there was a foggy mist that night. I pulled up to the gas pumps, and my wife went inside to get something to drink. The highway was deserted. There were no other cars on the street, and only one was parked in the back of the store, which I assumed belonged to the clerk. I stood outside and finished pumping gas, not paying attention to anything in particular. I watched my wife pay for her stuff and chat with the clerk inside when this weird sense came over me. You know, it's like a low noise that you can't hear, but you can feel it? Very eerie. I looked around, thinking that maybe someone started a big truck or something nearby that I couldn't see. It shook the ground somehow, but it was so low pitched that it made me feel queasy.

"My wife finished paying for her stuff, walked out the front door, immediately looked up, and froze. I was under the awning over the gas pumps, so I walked over to her and looked up. At first, I couldn't see anything. It took a moment to realize why. Above us, no more than a couple hundred feet, was a ship. I say ship because it was so huge it blotted out the entire night sky. It didn't have any lights on it, but we could see the bottom of this massive ship. It was dark gray against the street lights that illuminated it. That's how low to the ground it was, and it was moving very slowly. We could make out different areas like indentions in the hull, panels, openings, and what looked like section lines running along the bottom.

"We knew that it wasn't anything man-made. There's no way. Something that big would have to have had rocket engines propelling it, but it didn't. We couldn't make out any engines at all, but it was moving, slowly but surely.

"We watched it for a couple of minutes as it passed over, then just like that, it was gone; no more queasy feeling or sound pressure. It was just gone. We both saw it and can attest to that, but we never heard of anyone else reporting anything that night."

EPILOGUE

I have hunted small and large game most of my life. I've camped, ridden horses and four-wheelers, and hiked all over the country. It's a way of life that I have enjoyed as much as I have researched the cryptid creatures like Bigfoot. Whether one believes in Bigfoot or not, It's still an entertaining phenomenon. There are many theories as to what Bigfoot or Sasquatch may be. I've heard everything from spirit beings and aliens to flesh and blood or Nephilim. I tend to believe that Bigfoot is a flesh and blood creature. Elusive, yes, but still flesh and blood. I don't think it to be an alien, though many people claim to see strange and mysterious lights at the same time and location where Bigfoot is encountered. But, who knows? That's what makes the search for the truth so fun.

I travel to Honobia Creek a few times a year and have for several years now. I have traversed the Kiamichi Mountain range, diving into the deep canyons, climbing to the clear cut tops, and swam the river. The Kiamichi's are full of wildlife - gray foxes, coyotes, bobcats, turkeys, bears, and even mountain lions. Fish are plentiful in the creeks, ponds, and rivers. I have been so deep in the woods that one would think no human had ever gone before only to encounter a group of hikers. There have been many reported sightings of Bigfoot. Though I have combed those mountains, crisscrossing ridges, hunting, fishing the river and backwater creeks and ponds, I've never seen one.

ACKNOWLEDGEMENT

I would like to send a special thanks to the *"Lloyd Pye Foundation for Alternative Researchers."* Without their assistance and dedication to alternative research, this series would not be possible.

ABOUT THE AUTHOR

Paul G. Buckner is an Amazon Top 100 selling author, a Cherokee Nation citizen, musician, and an avid outdoorsman. He attended Northeastern State University and holds a bachelor's degree in Business Management and a Master's of Business Administration. He lives in Claremore with his wife Jody and son Chase.

Please visit Paulgbuckner.com to find other exciting books.

Printed in the USA
CPSIA information can be obtained
at www.ICGtesting.com
LVHW011734140324
774501LV00008B/382